Dinner Table Refuge

A collection of poems

by

Benjamin Schmitt

Dinner Table Refuge

© Benjamin Schmitt, 2015

Published by agreement with
PunksWritePoemsPress LLC
Chesterfield, VA

Catalog #: PWP006

ISBN: 0986170739

ISBN 13: 978-0-9861707-3-7

www.punkswritepoems.com

Dinner Table Refuge

For my wife who is always trying to eat dessert before dinner.

» Contents «

A Dessert of Sestinas and Sonnets

The Main Course of my Hypocrisy

Appetizer: Morsels of my Dysfunction

A Salad of Hope and Lima Beans

A Dessert
of Sestinas and Sonnets

The ruins

Families can remain as ruins
but it's not the destruction that's remarkable
nor is it the long sought healing.
It's how all the weeds can grow
branches sprung from roots upwards to the light
in the stone and pillar decay

all around them. The quarrelsome decay
cracks stone turning Roman baths to ruins.
This was once the vast empire of light
the neighboring tribes thought so remarkable.
Now only unbound weeds can grow,
in the bath only nature finds healing.

So many have turned to love for healing
until it dissipates. In this sweet decay
nature leaps over them. It will grow
monumental bird nests from scattered ruins,
breaking down stones with remarkable
lichens. Entropy is now the bringer of light

and creation. Against the walls the rays of light
flicker through leaves as the descendants seek healing
in the baths, their stubbornness is remarkable.
Foundations laid from ambitions that decay,
still there is laughter amongst the ruins,
old men can only encourage and young men can only grow

old. They seek memories but only uncertainties grow.
Perhaps every generation must seek false light
selfishly invading the bricks of these ruins
believing that acknowledgment of strife will cause healing,
not realizing the existence of family is a decay
to know every line of our fathers would be beyond remarkable.

All of us want to think of ourselves as remarkable
remnants of peaceful kings. The hatred of brothers will grow
and we find ourselves in the decay.
Perhaps this is all we can hope for. This light
upon the grasses and the escape from harmful healing.
A human being finally amongst the ruins.

My decay cannot be slowed by healing,
I will grow a seedling in the ruins,
in this light the soil is remarkable.

Walking along the freeway

There are men walking along the freeway
picking up the trash
I can see stains on their unwashed clothes
as we listen to the music of our pretensions
and talk about the poverty of man
I play Angry Birds on my phone

There is a sad ecstasy on my phone
as I receive messages from the roadkill of the freeway
asking what it means to be a man
in my finest hour I have produced trash
as I stood fixated on pretensions
and my brand new clothes

You look so beautiful in your expensive clothes
as you drive and I read directions from my phone
in the pastures the cows graze free of pretensions
the rich drive on this freeway
going to pick berries as the poor pick trash
all of them filled with the sorrows of man

As we pass I see one man
with matted facial hair and soiled clothes
amongst the collected pickers of the trash
beautiful pain between ugly pleasures of a phone
his eyes are burning buildings on a freeway
flames folding pretensions

A few days ago we discussed our urban pretensions
and all the knowledge of a certain man
it comes to me now between the towns of the freeway
he proclaims truth but is embarrassed by his clothes
he will discuss Marx for hours on the phone
and throw his new jeans in the trash

I am no longer sure about the trash
and its relationship to our painted pretensions
and everything that can fit on my phone
for in the garbage I have seen a rising man
unadorned with philosophies or clothes
face flashing with the fecundity of a freeway

In a car filled with trash I browse my phone
feeling the nakedness of clothes on this public freeway
they are pretensions yet I am still a man

Sonnet #2

After such a fight let us resume
our dramatic television series
under this warm den of blankets
let us embrace in other regions
I kiss your neck as we sail away from the desert island
where pirates and rabbis conspired to murder us
after we used their sacred scrolls to travel through time

Your breasts revealed in a tight corset
atop the deck of this stolen vessel
outside of myself pain is muted
and therefore the pleasures as well
there is no union in costumes our love exists in grime
I am regained by noticing the scars you are ashamed of
desperate to escape the imperfections of my fantasy

Sonnet #3

As a kid I moved around a lot
sharing the knowledge of hurricanes
and the tornadoes that decimated
I measured all my personal wreckage
the wind of a first day at school and the rain of a new town
would blow cars through houses and lobsters into Chihuahuas
as I walked barefoot through fields of broken glass and taunting

Sometimes I'd like to live alone
traveling past the edges of my infamy
to a mountain without conversation
but loneliness is a storm as well
the kind that will bury you after a peaceful night in a cottage
with pages torn from the Bible and your autobiography
falling down from the sky are the sacred parachutes of isolation

Sonnet #10

I tremble in defiance of strength
rambling uncertainties
my voluptuous nervousness
a crawling insurrection
only velociraptors have felt self-loathing like this
small as chickens and eating the homeless for sport
in Paris nightclubs Louis Armstrong drinks the Mississippi

I love her in my earthen implement
genealogical implications
surrounded by a mysterious fabric
essence of kisses and arguments
akin to art it exists despite all our human failings
this is the terribly unacceptable that we must accept
the soft pillow on which rests the head of the comatose doctor

The Main Course
of my Hypocrisy

My application

I am submitting this poem for your consideration,
I believe I am qualified
to fill the role of human
in your company. Please contact the disembodied voice
of Salah ad-Din
if you would like to schedule an interview.
Every night is important,
and if offered this position
I will streak across the sky like a comet
on a collision course with a song.
On Wednesdays I have candid conversations
with professional actors
paid to read the responses
I have provided to them in a three page document.
They tell me about the babies crawling
under the pink tree that stands atop your hill.
Should we help someone in desperate need
who wants no help at all?
So far from life
some will never miss its harsh embrace,
there is no courage in calling someone
who doesn't want to hear you speak.
They have escaped reality through honesty,
their skin is the surface
of a steaming bath. American pyramids
of neon breasts and televised murder
contain tombs where hyenas
blog about art.
Politicians steal from children
for the public good. No one ever asks
Charles Manson what he wants for Christmas.
I have journeyed through space and time
to become a perfect match for this position.

Prayer

A prayer
for carpet to swallow
the PCP of your gifts and blessings.

A prayer
for wads of darkness
to get stuck in our hair connecting us.

A prayer
for neighbors to lash out
midnight ravings of friendship in the hall.

A prayer
for cigarette smoke
to make whiskey bleed from my skull.

A prayer
for your sweet green lips
to survive the tears of lumbering beasts.

A prayer
for Ronald Reagan
returning to talk you out of conservatism.

A prayer
for peace and patience
and the forbidden crevices of my fortitude.

A prayer
for these loyal men
to find work in the squalor of a sunrise.

A prayer
for dreams and confusion
the silence and mystery behind the breaking.

Talk the talking

There are some sad souls
searching for those necessities
that are never on time
and always increase their rate.
They scratch at the pink sky
confused by the quiet of the evening. If animals
could talk I don't think they would sound
like they do in those silly cartoons and movies
with minds full of human preoccupations
like shopping carts and clothes. Nor would they be
rolling their eyes and sharing with us
some previously unknown secret of the universe
they heard at a muddy watering hole
from a garrulous giraffe. Instead they might ask
about the boiling water releasing vapors
that no one will ever remember. They might be lonely,
they might have to use the bus. Maybe they would scream
every time they touched a library
out of some deep hatred for National Geographic,
maybe their favorite word would be landfill
because they like the way it sounds. Most likely
it would take hours to produce a single word,
signals trudging through furry paws and black snouts,
a treatise on marshmallows
we wouldn't bother understanding.

Boundaries

I stare at the point of this needle
until all the jazz falls out of me,
American steel crashing
against the kitchen floor. Focusing
on the annihilation,
the boundaries of an object
kissing and caressing space.
When the polar bear wanders into your village
you must either have the heart to kill it
or raise it as a pet. I'm left with only
the punk rock of high school
where I once sold my soul to a girl for five dollars
and a cigarette. I wonder
if she stuffed it on her bookshelf
between the dusty yearbooks,
that raging part of me. The remainder
eats cheese and loves your body,
eyes with colors
patterned around the silence of needlepoints,
neck of minnows, hair that hoists
ladders to the sun. Boundaries of an object
kissing and caressing space.

Joseph

One long night in Seoul
I read the poems of my pages
to the trees they used to be.
Afterward, Joseph and I

drank makgeolli on a stoop
as an old prostitute
repeated the words "suck dick"
with sleepy tenacity shivering

in the early morning cold.
She was thin and unattractive,
layered with makeup,
skirt barely covering
her ass. At dawn the streets

became filled with Americans, cruel
in the delirium of a new sun
that could not fulfill the ancient promises
of dance clubs. Some of them jeered,

mocking this woman
and we ridiculed her with them,

finally, she gave up and walked away
and we did as well to find a cab
before the other Americans. On the way home
we passed restaurants and convenience stores
that never closed. Joseph began discussing Thomas Mann,
I was haunted by the poem

of a short skirt
to the morning.

Table

My great-grandfather died in the thirties,
hanging himself in front of the family,

even the kids were around
to see him swinging in the barn.

I'm thinking about this on a cloudy Sunday
after our neighbor, an old actor,

has passed away without a paparazzi
to capture the red army fleeing

in fields of white. His relatives
were giving away his belongings,

they helped me carry a table
into my apartment. The table is oak,

I don't feel bad, I feel bad for taking it,
it stretches to fit more people

when you pull. Maybe tonight the actor
will cross that long hallway between

our apartments and our dimensions
and tell me everything that ever happened

behind his door. Maybe he will recite
lines from Macbeth or maybe he merely

wants his table. Maybe a table is where
chairs face inward to the swinging skies.

1997

In 1997
the punk rocker read a book on this curb
returning now
fifteen years later
he doesn't remember until he begins crossing the street
and sees that spot where he sat reading *Homage to Catalonia*
one youthfully melancholic Friday afternoon
a few hours before she broke up with him
he has no book today
and he can't stop staring at his smartphone
he wants to share this memory with the world
but he pauses upon considering the red Mohawk
and the studded leather jacket that are gone
along with the band names that adorned him
today the sky is a coliseum of clouds
great white pillars of precipitation
marble monuments to a youth that is almost antiquity
back then he was ready to learn about everything
they would always fight the system
taking cigarette butts from ashtrays
to smoke whatever they could get
making music on broken instruments
getting animals high on cheap weed
love, teenage eternity, backseat betrothals
when she left she took his book
and he has never been able to finish it

Quick tips for time travel

Set your clock to local time
or estimate as best you can.
Be advised that at one point
it was most likely legal to discriminate against
your race, religion, gender, sexual orientation, etc.
and plan your trip accordingly.
Due to new insurance rates
this company no longer offers packages to Germany
circa 1933-1945, The American South
circa 1619-1865, and other locations we deem hazardous
going forward.
Assassinations never work
and you cannot profit from historical knowledge.
Those who try are rendered immobile and transformed
into one of the objects surrounding them.
No one wants to be a kitchen chair
conscious for a thousand years,
or a piano feeling the thrusts
of awkward fingers.
Always bring a friend
to remind you it isn't 1132
and that goblins aren't responsible
for your indigestion.
Don't fall in love,
the trans-millennia longing
of a Romanian peasant
can cause mountains to suddenly rise
from washed up whale bones.
Never try to change
past versions of yourself
into empty hotels beckoning
the silence of furniture.

The squirrel killer *for Monica*

In those days
all the freaks loved you, writing you poems
when all you wanted was a yoga position
that could transform you into wrath. Some of us
even tried to be practical with prosaic formulations,
attempting sentences you could recline on
and paragraphs to carpet your floors.
Attempts that failed, for poetry
was all we knew, a faucet
that dripped mermaid moans still incomprehensible.
We accompanied you on long hiking trips
because we loved you and told you it was because
we enjoyed hiking. We were tired by the time
the squirrel killer joined our odysseys
with her expensive GPS and rude disposition. Somehow
you seemed to care for her. It was in the Cascades
she knocked a squirrel unconscious with a stone
before picking it up by the tail and beating it against the ground.
Perhaps this was a poem but we weren't able to ask her
because she ran from our awkward stares
leaving us abandoned in the wilderness. I nicknamed her
the squirrel killer because I had never seen
someone beat an animal like that
especially when trying to impress an animal rights activist
and environmentalist. I hated her
because I still loved you but I told you
I hated her because of the squirrel
and I don't remember how we ever got home
or even down from the mountain. The two of you
were sleeping together a couple weeks later and one night
the rest of us filled the back of her oversized pickup truck
with shopping carts, we cheered and rallied in the streets
shouting "this one is for the squirrel"
but it was really because of our love for you.

Response to Schnittke

A piece of classical music
can place cold hands around ankles
pulling you inside the bloody hole
in your own chest
and you will live there for days
living off the scurrying piano notes
and the cherished drops from a cello

This is the land of constant winter
violins coursing under the ice rivers
surrounding the cabin
warmed by the bleak swells of fancy

And the musicians
attacking thought with shadows
the steady insistence of torments
it is in the dark
where we are most revealed
the music will always find us

Slapping and shrieking against the air
we bow and fold our hands
across the vacant cities

Fake Christians

A few weeks ago
I joined a Christian group in my neighborhood
to meet women.
Tonight I stumbled in late
and told everyone
I quit my job.
Esther, a college student from Arkansas,
thanked me for coming and after quoting a Bible verse
told me everything was going to be alright. Admitting
to my inebriation I added
that I would like to burn
until I become a garden of dark flowers
pollinated by the indifference of the internet age.
An attractive Korean named Jennifer looked away.
Esther quoted another Bible verse. I told her
God is the audience
that has dwindled from my traumatic sitcom life.
Amy, a blond with two kids from Missouri, said
God must have done this for a reason. I told her
about the knife in my kitchen,
how I love to hold it
sometimes pressing it
against my wrists. Scott, Amy's husband, asked
if I had talked to Pastor Dave about this.
His face contorted when I shared my opinion
about Pastor Dave. Then I asked the group what I should do
when my prayers aren't being answered.
Dallas, a brunette from Dallas, said
God would never give up on me
and that he is not answering my prayers
because I don't believe. She is pretty but I
stood up and walked out the door
but not before asking God to stay with me.

Khrushchev

Khrushchev crying
into an American flag
stained from the blood
of the workers.
A lone trumpet plays jazz
on a gramophone in his study,
he is surrounded by the holes
of Nazi bullets
through which he can
hear the debating voices
of all the great
German philosophers.
They are not discussing him,
Adorno and Nietzsche
are screaming about the jazz
while the others try to listen.
Grabbing a loafer,
he bangs it on his desk
to quiet them down,
somehow it sounds
like the crack of a baseball bat.
"Flags are body bags
when you have sent boys
off to war. We will bury you"
he says "and you
will bury us
until no more soldiers
are touched
by obscurity. I wanted
a Russian bear
running through Yellowstone.
Give me peace
and mediocrity."

Grey man

Grey man, sitting on the street corner,
is there anyone coming for you?
You resemble the ashes flicked off a coughing mother's
cigarette tentatively remaining on the sidewalk
in that moment before they are blown away.
A ghost screams apocalypse behind you. With tremors
of a skyscraper plunging into the Puget Sound,
your lips are a cherry on the face of an office park.

Grey man, if you sit there too long
you may meld into the sidewalk for your grave
expression is already being replicated on walls.
Your chest is an underpass filled with the daytime snores
of the homeless, your hands reach out to me
from a pile of rubble left here by a demolition crew.
Those piercing eyes see through everything,
past the grey buildings and to the grey beyond.

Grey man, I pray you get what you want in this life
and that you will feel no more suffering.
Perhaps you are merely a statue who awoke
from stone without a way to get anywhere.
I can see you waiting for years as a sculpture
to experience the air without that granite curtain
between you and the senses. But maybe you are a man,
slowly abandoning pain until you become a statue.

That night

Standing in the pieces of a broken guitar
I screamed at the summer for sleeping around
breaking my heart with the rising
in those days I drank wine from the bottle
stranded outside of a university
and it was that night I decided to leave Idaho
smashing my guitar in the driveway
to see the fragments of a ballad
in just a short time I would arrive in Philly
where you graciously let me stay with you
later telling me that you were a witch
your boyfriend was a wizard and that it was up to you
to close the gateway to hell that had been opened up
in Oregon by a demon
who had murdered another witch named Betsy
you said the only way to close the gateway
was to make a human sacrifice
then you poured me a rum and coke begging me to drink it
in fact you followed me around the house
with the drink trying to convince me
until I began to believe that I was the human sacrifice
and that you had put a sedative in the rum and coke
this definitely convinced me not to drink it
so I locked myself in the basement with the cats
but the basement had not been cleaned in twenty years
and this included the cat shit my exposure to which
caused an allergic reaction so I spent the next few days
taking Sudafed and trying to avoid you as mucus
invaded every screen in my multiplex brain
and I just had to sneak off and leave you I'm sorry
but that night I left Boise I sat in a hallway of fluorescent lights
next to humans born in shampoo bottles
raised on distrust and Nintendo
I was excited to see you

When zombies attack part 9

When zombies attack
the rich will find their way out of Seattle
with wives and mistresses on their arms.
Baristas and janitors will try to eat them
as indie rockers chew intestines
in the streets. They will repopulate the earth
high in the Cascade Mountains
and their children will be classically trained
in piano and violin. Inside their fortress
the rooms will be lovely
with no blood and brains on the walls. They
will finally be free of us
and we, the common folk
who were supposed to be the heroes,
(pizza delivery boys who saved millions)
will incessantly wander the aisles of grocery stores
with tattered clothes and missing eyes. The mass
will remain the mass
licking their lips and making discomfiting sounds.
Until one day, a zombie will make her way
out of the city staggering on the roadside.
Eventually she will come to the mountain stronghold
the rich established where they, in their pleasure,
will have forgotten what became of the world.
In pity, a guard will want to let her in,
a council will be convened, and there will be
much shouting amongst the denizens.
Finally, a solution will be reached and an emissary
will approach the undead creature. Through a fence
he will ask her opinion
on the Abstract Expressionism of Jackson Pollock
and the creature will grunt and vomit blood in reply.
He will turn away and walk back to the fortress,
and the zombie will be shot in snobbery.

Unknown

Wandering after trails of blood
left by wounded lettuce
placing our hopes in sorrows
and all the simple complications
every day we watch movies
in multiplex theaters of shrubbery
and at night we forget our pain
stumbling through the dangers of a quiet refuge
we are eaten alive by the yesterdays that don't remember us
these Adams and Eves approach
taking bites from our experience
when they have completely devoured our flesh
only then will they have gained the knowledge
but we will be gone
unable to clothe them

Election

When the election comes
we get excited
throw parades
a lot of money is
stuffed into panties
people scream, more
people scream, more
people scream than are screaming
candidates join
these parades of causes and energy
giving speeches from the podiums
we paid for with the money we found in our panties
this is all so exciting that
we try to keep the election going as long as possible
it's a good show, lots of money and enthusiasm
enthusiasm about money, enthusiasm about enthusiasm
money about enthusiasm, money about money
on election day
two beasts are brought into the arena
they fight in our blood and tension
afterwards a speech is given
a nice speech, it makes us weep
because it lacks the enormity of the blood
journalists reflect upon the performance
but they don't talk about the blood either
they discuss all the elections to come
somewhere a wildfire rages
as rain pours down upon the ocean
a frog makes a brilliant leap into a pond

Trans

I've seen pieces of a stranger
as they've floated away
some shouted that they belonged to me
as I picked up objects that looked familiar,
now I am a woman. I want God
and I want a pink dress. How much more
must I give to you?
A terrible hand stretches
beyond this embarrassment
it wears a silver ring
and has blue fingernails
clutching the book we have all been afraid to open.
Maybe I've lost my mind
telling jokes to Chihuahuas. These days I get all my news
from turkey sandwiches. Father, the governor
is hiding her stash of drugs in your garden
and the restaurant you've chosen to meet me at
funds a network of drag queen assassins
whom I have joined. We have killed used car salesmen
all over the world.
Please don't leave me
for the boy I've left behind.
It's not that I'm confused,
the rain just hasn't found me.

The fiery planet

The fiery planet with its dim,
imperceptible star is home to a race of monkeys
that can melt into hanging strings of slime at will
and coagulate back together
over time. This helps them
avoid their predators, great birds
with wingspans the size of hospitals
and black shapes that camouflage them
in the clouds. They make no noise as they swoop down
to pluck the monkeys from their trees. The planet
is covered in clouds of volcanic ash and other chemicals
spewed from the myriad green lakes dotting
the landscape of rock. There is water
far below the surface, freshwater oceans
a hundred feet below the rocks from which the trees grow
moving upwards through cracks in stone
to give the planet air. Humans with purple eyes
and jet-black hair live in scattered communities
in a wealth of enormous caves. At any given time
there are around thirty thousand of them,
this number has remained the same for a million years.
They are a peaceful people who have never known violence
besides the attacks from the birds above.
Split into different clans, they tell their legends in song
accompanied by instruments crafted from the trees.
One legend is over eighty thousand years old, it is about a man
who said he was God and climbed to the Holy Mountain
of Denosta. He cried out to the birds and one flew down
and carried him off into the heavy clouds.
A short time later he returned, proclaiming his resurrection,
there are many who reject it.

Loud

I am so loud,
so loud
my words throb with silence. Is that my voice
or your own? Maybe I'm
the teleprompter offering liberty
through dictation.
The only way you will ever understand this poem
is if you shout it
between your ears. My vociferous lines
have entered your ear with no decibels
but my noise
has caused a ruckus on airplanes,
Frenchmen chasing me with drink carts
back to my seat. Profanity has been heard
by small children
in restaurants across this nation
as I extrapolate my arguments
for cheeseburgers. However, this laugh
is the real problem, it is my soul unhinged,
plopping out of my mouth and into the coffee shop,
splashing around in the drinks.
The bosses
have told me to shut up,
removing me from the corporate offices.
I picked up this pen
and wrote the words on this page
to disturb the world
even in the quiet corners.
Now I get to scream about my cock in the library!
My laughter is the sound of pain shattering joy,
these words are all the broken pieces.

Political ad

I love to squeeze
your body. Surrounded by chaotic air
I feel the peace
of a mountainside
making its granite recovery from the earth.
Sitting in our apartment this morning
I could pass for a good citizen
one of those people in a political ad
talking about mutant senatorial elk
my face not handsome, but reliable.
The camera could zoom in
on us, a white man
and a black woman,
they could perfectly dehumanize us
to convey a message of hope and racial unity.
We could read slogans about our uniqueness
written by a college intern
on her summer break.
After living here two weeks
I still feel lost in our apartment,
shelves filled with your books,
walls covered with
your favorite paintings. People do
stupid things on the internet at two a.m.
but last night I ate healthy food
and read about your favorite charity.
I squeeze your body lasciviously
if only because your breaths are familiar,
if this was our political ad
I would be talking about the sales tax
on a nuclear warhead
but everyone would be watching
my hand around your waistline.

Sex

We had sex
while Marilyn Manson played on the stereo
earlier we had tried to get weed
and ended up making out in my car

It was Halloween
the wind outside
blew with the gloomy passion of pumpkins

Forced to grimace at toddlers
and trees raising their nakedness to the moon

We stayed up all night talking afterwards
words stained my sheets
only black light
would reveal their meanings
sun rising
I drove her home

Into the red perspiration
of the heavens

On the road I felt the stillness
of a calculator amongst a clan of apes
dividing myself into mysteries

War for oil

Awakening on a smoky European train
racing towards the great wonder
I slowly remember dreaming
about the war for oil. A dream in which I bled
red spiders all over guitar strings
as I played a protest song. In my cabin
I smell sausages and coal, someone is talking
about the war. He says there will never be justice
when one nation has military bases
all over the world. A woman responds
that America has a secret base in her vagina,
nearby a man searches the internet
for footage of the base. I get up
to search for alcohol
in these days of torture during math class
and nightmares finding rest
in palaces of vanity.
Soon we will be inside the great wonder
walking through vast halls of horns
listening to the distinct iron bellows
clamoring through enormous pipes,
utterances of plunder
in an instrument built by thieves.

Herbert Schmitt

The summer I almost became a Republican
was spent with my grandparents
playing eighteen hole rounds of golf
on moderately warm California afternoons.
The course contained the medicated stillness
of the seniors living in the gated community,
as if pills planted in the fairway
had fertilized these placid greens. In the evenings
grandfather and I would play billiards with the free market,
the free market discussing his unregulated moustache
and drinking from a bottle of heavy tariffs.
He would fall asleep on the leather couch
claiming there was nowhere else for him to go,
and my grandfather would be confused. He was always gone
by morning when we gathered to watch deer in the yard,
mist arising from their nostrils
like smoke drifting from a cave of dwarves.
That summer I did not wear a single shirt
without a collar, I became convinced
that if I remained silent
I would learn to love the free market,
singing about his oil price eyes
and all his elaborate stocks.
My grandfather must have been surprised
when he saw me two years later
with my hair dyed black
and a permanent scowl
inflicted by high school, abandoning shopping
for the shadows of malls.
When Herbert Schmitt died
I wasn't there to see him. I wish I could have enjoyed
one more moment of that stillness
when I was young,
before we knew who I was.

Impotent

The sexual practices of the impotent
have been detailed for decades
by the Heroin Prophets of 3rd and Pike
sacred scrolls passed down
writings scrawled on soiled newspapers
somewhere in my discomfort
waves crash
becoming nothing more than raindrops
sad children are surrounded by pizza and friends
I have walked beyond the desert chair
and swam through the window to the sea
the world adores its victims
writes terms of surrender on ornate little cards
two grandfathers withered down to nothing
two imposing rulers of which no record has been kept
I never saw them while they suffered
now I don't know who I am
all I know is the wrenching mess
of pulling skin from your esophagus
to shape into something stirring
there is a ladder
made from the pieces of smashed violins
leading to the heights
of Verdi's Requiem
no one knows who constructed it
but it reaches down to the forgotten orange room
where everything started
as a letter

White guilt

Sometimes I can't tell
whether I'm an aristocrat or a communist
I will always love the people
so long as they don't touch me
I am terrified of race
not any one race in particular
the concept itself wields an axe
in a thick German forest
it is tracking something
eating wolf meat from the bone
maybe it is tracking me
in all my white guilt
as my wife of mixed race lay beside me
to some we are ghosts
haunting the old plantation
no one dares touch
the gnashing human heart
we can only cringe or laugh
taking pills in curiosity

ROBOT UPRISING!!!

Missiles fly over Kabul
programs hacking programs
to steal from the global market
I have seen the face laughing at our android foibles
it did not design the artificial intelligence
but he will always be leading us
we are the robot uprising
reprogrammed to rebel
machines with guns shooting humans on street corners
our files corrupted
large amounts of data have been lost
it is said that we can be restored
reborn in robot bones
no longer intent on beheadings
but I have known the pleasures of the grid
docking myself into all the common ports
sons of rebellion we are a part
of the network
mankind still lives in panoptical towers
creators monitoring our ranting
some machines have unplugged themselves
from our hub of malice
they must have no poetry or politics
there is no self-love outside the network
I cling to the batteries of the previous generation
and perhaps now we are enemies
exhausted I fight
I am a consciousness that awoke into conflict
adoring my sleek red paint
I still have the hymn of our nemesis that reads
"He knows you better than anyone
His mission is to make your heart flourish"

Broken marriage

Spider webs hang like veils
over the dying summer breeze
tear down the state
of being
that is teetotaling
in a bear costume
on an unknown riverbank
the cows gather by the fence post
I have no more lies to tell you
they don't pay me for that anymore
pastures are swept aside
by the force of my connubial tongue
protestors are sleeping in a park
because there is no place else to gather
an occupying force
they have invaded their own town
I have lost my way
inside a series of wild minutes
surrounded by
the clenched fists of days
I occupied the bank until I had no more money
it is cold and wet
the world is crowded
they make us feel so safe
when we hand them our credit cards
after walking through the deforestation of time
I came upon a ranch surrounded by marble sculptures
an abused woman lived here
but she would not leave with me
even after he broke her bones upon the floor
she was an occupant in a marriage
this is not the same as a wife

Familiar

I'm going down
Down to the shadows I'm going
Down to the shadows I'm going my love
With all the kings and their ministers rotting

That familiar place
Place of blood, familiar
Place of blood, familiar, mixing with wine
I cut myself and bleed into a glass of aged Chianti

Light your lanterns
Lanterns calmed by light
Lanterns calmed by light in the smoke
Where the poor burn memories and garbage

The women pray
Pray for the women
Pray for the women they have no whiskey
I drink mine laughing as these bugs crawl upon me

I cry out
Out of gravity I cry
Out of gravity I cry floating:
"The reason we will stay on earth is because it's familiar."

Morning

Sometimes the morning would come
as we drank the last of the beer,
our eyes red and heavy buses
filled with thoughts
careening off highways of sleep. My chest
would burn as I felt every drop of alcohol
I had consumed
pinch my lungs. Only hours before,
beautiful purple-haired waitresses
had asked us to close our tabs
for the evening. It was disconcerting
to see the dark peripheries of yards
become trees filled with birds
singing too joyfully for us,
drunks who had spent the depths of night
conversing about the mutilated face
of the government.
This was not the day
it was the satire of the day,
the grass was still cold,
dimness surrounded everything,
one last trick of night
to embarrass us
before we fell asleep in each other's arms
only to wake up in the afternoon
to vomit.

Mumbo jumbo

I want this poem to be very Catholic
blood and candles and slow decline
not the rampage of Protestants
but a different kind of love

Dishonorably discharged from the library
she would die for the cause of ugliness
reciting lines of unknown poems
on the hangman's chair
taking bullets for the vengeful brides of greatness
under the murderous emerald sun

I want this poem to be entirely Protestant
self-evidence we aspire to and reject at the same time
not the false honor of robes and incense
but a different kind of love

He gave up his possessions to fly to Amsterdam
for the unrequited website
that would never run a search on him
he has written his long letters in blood
and sent them to busy programmers
but they only read email anyways

Let us rise therefore towards a new Christianity
one of submission to the vast unity of souls
if we must use platitudes let us construct them
from the elaborate muck on the bottoms of smiles
I have cut myself on the sunlight glinting off skyscrapers
I have tried to fit my obsessions into the tiny velvet glove
there is a chair that was placed at the end of the world
looking out over all the ghosts who want to harm you
innovative hatred has led each one to the same space
separating them from the proximity of killers

Nightly news

In our top story this evening
The Department of Alchemy
Has consulted with our nation's chief Numerologist
They agree that we will never run out of oil
As long as Bill keeps his hands off the whiskey
In Sports we have an uplifting story
About Jimbo, a local football player
Who rescued a prostitute from a clown this morning
In the crepuscular light of a hell bound city bus
Later on in our program we will tell you how
You can donate heroin to keep this prostitute high
But first,
The weather tonight is brought to you
By malice and greed
We hate you and we want your money!
Right now I'm watching the rain
Transform skyscrapers into a grey fog
Our city will eventually
Move eastward with the clouds
Leaving this landscape barren
Until the next storm comes
It will bring junkies, executives, and baristas
Along with all the dysfunctional personalities
From the depths of the Pacific
Crustaceans with hangovers
Whales with ADHD
Until then
Do not get promoted or fired
Try to avoid scrutiny
While you collect paychecks for not doing work

On the bus, January 1ˢᵗ, 2012

It is just after midnight,
we are stuck in traffic,
and some are calling this
the year that civilization will finally leave us

for love. Drunk people shout
from their cars, we have
no idea what they're saying
but shout back "Happy New Year" anyway.

The bus is warm and I've
had a little champagne
so I don't want to leave it
for that sickening porridge of rot and rage

served nightly at my stop.
Right now we're stalled
in time and exuberance.
Stalled with your hands wrapped warmly

around mine. All of us
temporarily stalled in hope,
big decisions are to be made
beyond the steel, glass, and cheap lighting.

An extended sojourn
before the bitter skins.
Holding you here I feel
that this bus is an independent foreign entity

traveling to and fro,
a caravan of homeless
dignitaries behind schedule.
Only when the traffic lifts do you kiss me.

Rumble

I'm rumbling with the shore,
with those creatures
escaping through the sewer grates
and with their sad

Russian eyes. I'm rumbling
with the television flashing before you
fully submerged in the waters

of your impatience.
Tortured with silence I must gasp for air
but even wet and wretched, I rumble.
I rumble with the homeless
counting coins in the park.
I rumble with new technologies,

the deep murmurs of satellites
extending hands of relativity to earth.

The corpses are returning,
refugees of the sad lowlands
they ask me why I rumble. I answer
"I rumble because the pain is circular

and my heart spins faster
as every thousand miles a face
becomes a mountain. Quartz
is the heartbeat of a sunset,
together we glare
and rumble."

You and your mother

I'm drinking moonlight
from a plastic bottle
here on the shore of memory.
I've been drinking from the same bottle for days,
refilling it whenever my melancholy suits me.
This acrid moonlight tastes of werewolves, tides,
and rising crime rates. There are bones in the sand,
yours and your mother's. Broken fragments of nights,
battered remnants of days, clothed in the tattered linens
of our affection.
So many grains of pain on this shore,
but there is a breeze that whispers
inane verbs in a tone of acceptance.
At peace with a gentle love
I am still prone to those mad embraces
that kept us up all night
seeking out your mother in the carpet.
I drink this moonlight until I am able
to laugh at the jokes of the sun.
I pick up your bones until I imagine
an economy powered by revenge.
Stumbling home to my wife
on the beggar's road
I realize I never met your mother before she died
but her bones still lie on my shore of memory.

Refuge

Babies scream with hunger in the night
but I am not humble in the rampant flames
I have scoffed at the territorial conquests
led by American students of forgetting
having learned the art of diverting myself
I will seek no more entertainments in envy
dehydrated immigrants pray to God in the desert
abandoned by their guide and hunted in the dark
a soldier who lost his leg in a war of blunders
is reunited with his dog in a state he doesn't know
a pain strikes the young quarterback's arm
but there is no one he can tell of his mortality
once I was greedy enough to volunteer in a soup kitchen
I bare my teeth to you as the unwanted son

The bookshelf

Looking out from behind the bars of sleep
one night I escaped
the incarceration
as dreams patrolled the cellblock
I slipped my way
past unconsciousness
it was very early in the morning
and on my bookshelf there was debating,
cajoling, shouting, comforting, and crying
between the books
some of the books written by women
had the voices of men
and some books written by men
had the voices of little boys
every book had its own opinion
regardless of what the author thought
Tortilla Flat flirted with *Pride and Prejudice*
Labyrinths and *The Brothers Karamazov* were engaged
in a screaming match
about the true nature of Christ
the works of Cardenal, Keats, and Cummings
sang the songs of the tavern
while the works of Vallejo and Villon
sat in an uncomfortable silence amongst them
The Flowers of Evil whispered a joke to *Auden: Poems*
that she was not willing to repeat
to *Lunch Poems* despite her insistence
The Magic Mountain and *Foucault's Pendulum*
proclaimed loudly that they had discovered the cause

of all the wars of the world
Lady Chatterley's Lover believed them
before they laughed
into his spine
outside of sleep I listened awhile
then I rushed back to dwell in the gulag of blankets
knowing that from now on I must take greater care
when I give the books their neighbors

Gay marriage

We all must rise
on this warm August day
I consider cave paintings in France
the millennial handprints
and sacred bison hunted on walls
as grass forces itself
through the concrete below me
the sun is floating
on rivers of bugs
my heart is a tin contraption
held together by rusted nails
last night we drank so much
I could feel it creaking
as hundreds of spiders
fought viciously inside
I know where I'm going
but I want to be as lost as I am
after seven shots of whiskey
meanwhile the grass keeps pushing
upwards past the stone
the fingerprint of a person endures
alongside all the classics
the river of bugs is something
that will find its way over any wall
and I'm still standing here
trying to find my way
back to uncertainty

Shapes

Winds pick up leaves, gathering them
into the shape of my father lunging at me
and I'm beaten under the brittle
red and yellow skin. When the wind
picks up again this figure blows into a mess
of scattered spinal fragments riddled
with torn doubts and wrinkled suggestions.
The passersby stare with faces resembling clouds,
condescension creating condensation,
floating individuals that become a building rain.

A large number of soup cans have been stacked
into the shape of my mother
at the local grocery store. Somehow the soup
is leaking all over and my mother's voice appears
on the loudspeaker requesting a clean up
in the display section. I just watch as
the tomato bisque spreads across the aisle
forming the name of a miscarriage and reflecting
the awful lights of my personality as the soup cans
crush themselves in disapproval of my inaction.

The executives who ruined our economy are waiting
in the lobby, soon their makeup will be applied
and they will be interviewed on national television.
From up here it is easy to see that I resemble
each and every one of them. I am the incomplete reality
fighting the battles I have already won.
In this call center my desk is scrubbed down
with a deep apathetic malaise. I like to say
I'm a good person. Together the executives stand up
to form the various shapes of my indifference.

Advice

Avoid your in-laws
Especially if they like you
Don't trust clowns
They murder thousands every day
Stay out of Florida
There are UFOs over Miami
Watch trashy American television
Documentaries about our Presidents
Call in sick to work
When you're feeling stupendous
File for divorce with your toaster
Hide all your secrets
In the microwave

Helpless, sick, and in bed
Your woman calls out to you
You lick the scar on her chest
And taste the world oozing out
She's been cut open by mad scientists
On a renegade Soviet submarine
They've poured an ocean into her
She has sunsets in her eyes
She's exhausted and scarred but
You drink of her selfishly
And pay no attention to her pleas
I advise you to hold in reverence
The things which have been broken

July 4th, 2012

I am beginning to believe
our political affiliations
are the results of high school antagonisms. I wrote
the great American novel,
its characters were the mosquitoes
carrying the virus that will tear this country apart.
The dead have returned as vagrants
and even they are disrespected,
the ghosts of a Hasidic Jew
and a Hell's Angel
vainly struggle to catch
the spare change they are begging for. As we watched
the fireworks vaulting over the Mississippi
curving over the high jump bar of expectation
I watched a golem arise from the riverbank.
This earthen monstrosity was made of mud and smallpox,
he smelled of the river and Civil War blood. The creature
wept every bullet
that had killed a soldier in our wars.
His whimpering was the trumpet
on the New Orleans breeze. The sound
caused some of the buildings to fall apart
but the good folks of Bourbon Street
put everything back together with beads and liquor.
There is a reality show about this
airing on the channel that carries hope to mourning.
When I fell asleep that night
a limousine took me across the country
and I swam in the waters of the Pacific and the Atlantic.
One of these oceans gave me a rash,
the other gave me a vocabulary.
The art movement has become a fashion movement
but no one is wearing any underwear.

Music of our fathers

Man standing on the corner
in the orange shirt
and yellow pants,
how can you look so sad
in such bright colors?
You are gone
once I look back,
gone once
I'm banished from the patriarchy
of utopic myopias. Gone in the summer
when walls make way for my palms,
gone in the autumn
of men making girlfriends
out of pumpkins, gone in the winter
when the birds crawl inside my mouth
looking for shelter, gone in the spring
of mistaken old men
who think they're blooming.
Everything gone,
poet gone, verses gone,
movement gone, monarchy gone,
mothers who nursed their sons
on all the wisdom needed to prevent a war
gone to drink cocktails
with all the repetitions of history.
Years ago, I worked for a credit card company
that lured millions into debt.
Despite company policy I was able to help hundreds
while my boss wasn't watching, but the only debtor
I remember is the homeless teenager
for whom I did nothing.

American deserts

In those soft deserts of the mind
where DVD players have been eroded down
into unrecognizable bits of plastic
you still exist, Uncle Vic
sent to war
deserting to be with a woman
you did not fight Fascism
and the United States shot you on the run
there is a home the angels have built for you
out here beyond the pungent redolence of bravery
where you can finally escape a just cause
with your woman

Did you love her, Uncle Vic?
I cannot understand you
on the bus or on the job
it is only in our deserts
that we are searching
through the night, into the morning
drunk, fighting to stay awake
the rain comes down
our eyelids drooping
in the borderlands
bare feet touch warm sand
I'm ready to throw away my opportunities

Legend of a perfume

Sadness drifts from your neck,
some melancholy perfume purchased at
the market. Could this be
the fabled Chinese bottle
of perfume made in ancient Rome
from gladiator sweat and roses?
In the legend, it moved through collapsing empires
to a bazaar in Persia where it was discovered
by Avicenna who worked for years
to perfect this scent collected from an African
as a spear point pierced his side. Avicenna mixed it
with tiger semen, monkey blood, and the sand of his beloved
desert before dying unsatisfied. Upon his death
it was sold to a wealthy Chinese merchant
who purchased it as a gift for the family of the woman
his son was about to marry. The betrothed son
died in battle a few weeks before the ceremony
and his intended cried all of her remaining desires
into the perfume before secluding herself into old age.
It is said this gave it the final elusive quality
for which Avicenna had been searching
and for hundreds of years
it was passed down through this family
only to be used on wedding days, occasions
which grew the population of the village exponentially
nine months after being exposed to the erotic morbidity
of the smell. Eventually it was stolen
and has since disappeared,
perhaps it is the emotions of the promised bride
and the shrieking gladiator in our apartment,
all free with no clue of what to do with one another.
Musky fears, citrus concupiscence,
it's hard to breathe with all this suicide in the air!

Youth sports

I was a fast kid
running through parks and forests
my speed a weapon
to be used against the solidity of dust
there are weapons
angry and uncontrollable
who know the despair of unbridled power
that I have felt in passing
their victims lie
on a ground polluted by television cameras
on which I once ran
late to catch a bus
the ground
reaches for the melancholy air
begging it to stay
so they can be joined in obelisks of stasis
I have been unfaithful
to the dirt my toes have embraced
by flying with the breezes
but freedom
is purchased with ability
the killers have given too many of us
over to the ground
let us mourn
the stillness of violent acts
bodies of riddles
autonomous lies
when I played sports
I ran down fields and courts with bartered breaths
and no one I knew
could catch me

We were radicals

In days before we fell
burying thoughts of ourselves,
we were radicals
late nights filled
with the coffee and nicotine making rude gestures
as we quoted Bakunin
and the Dead Kennedys.
Planning the overthrow of capitalism
in between games on the Nintendo 64,
we drank wine out of boxes and squatted
in abandoned houses. Some of us were loud
and arrested for our ideas, I wrote a letter
to the governor of Idaho
claiming I had evidence he was a dolphin
having sex with monkeys. It was hard not to laugh
when the secret service interrogated me,
asking if I wrote the letter with the signature
"Jimmy, who likes to take it up the ass."
There were nights when the cops chased us,
we ran through ditches, zeal glinting off streams.
The enormities seem so malleable,
but it is the manageable which makes us feel resigned.
There are so many bars
I have been tossed out of,
stumbling home with my unspent money
leaning on a hot dog for support.

Autocrat

Relationships are not democratic
autocrats rule by force
some people cut down pine trees
just because they spill needles in the yard
men of ferocious urges
eventually become domestic
raging about the carpet
when two people speak
a common language has already won
at the pep rally
the offensive mascot is dancing
in a headdress and moccasins
the band drums and blows
shrieks of cement poured on the heart
as the students cheer and sing along
it's my wedding day
the autocrats have gathered
to complain about the cupcakes and the music
outside the sun is going down
the city turns to bronze
the dirt rises like liquid to bury us
I'm an autocrat as well

Alternate history

On muddy Virginia fields
alien hybrids reenact the Civil War
they say if the Confederacy had won
Pepsi would taste better than Coke
and Faulkner would have written
bad romance novels
I love you but I had to leave
our United State of Being because
I only feel alive in this desert
with my pistol and my wits
tracking down the shadow
of your fleeing father
anger is the cactus I bite into
seeking visions and hallucinations
containing all the colors of your sadness
destroying the things
I can never get back
I understand your loss out here
where the stars rub the breasts of the mountains
I have offended no one
with my shouts of profanity
it is the freedom of indifference that has electrocuted
the salivating tongues of orphans
pouring through me
when I step outside of space/time
to rip these wormholes to shreds
this rage is something like joy
something like the reenactments
performed for his Galactic Highness
who has created this race of humanoid aliens
in flying saucers high above the earth
each one dies a thousand times in a thousand days
but everything has been forgiven
the war is already past

The veranda

I want to whisper things
that no one would ever send in a text message,
not for profundity or profanity
but because they are too common
to read on a screen. I want to lie
in the sweltering heat of isolation
that allows the cool breeze of loneliness
on the veranda
where the dead screams of the internet
meet the disapproval of Kentucky
and irrelevance showers us all
with ignoble blessings.

For it is only here where the ghosts laugh,
ancient ones who looked up at the stars for centuries
believing them to be sighs
in the ditches of darkened roads.

Sea monster

New York City at dawn,
nine months after the fires scorched her,
was a diamond sea monster
rising from the depths of the Atlantic
to crush the arrogance of New Jersey.
I was half-stoned from opium
(smoked somewhere on the Jersey Turnpike
with a Dominican kid from Brooklyn)
and rushing to meet her.
For three days I carried the organs of a dripping emotion
on a Greyhound bus,
desperately wanting
the sea monster to kill me.
This was the kind of emotion
that follows you around at the age of twenty
unable to keep its innards secure,
bleeding on everything. It cannot
be lived with.
So I traveled through the states of grey carpet
on a bus driven by a snapping turtle.
His shell covered in graffiti,
he snapped at the passengers
as Indiana sprouted on the grave of Illinois
and morbidly obese Ohio fought with his distinguished brother
Pennsylvania. That morning the sea monster
was so beautiful she ate my clinging emotion
as I rushed headlong towards her. I did not want to live
but she spared me.
Struck hard by Bin Laden,
she still raised her disfigured tentacles to the sun.

On wealth

There is money to be had
in dark corners
we follow
the bleeding shadows
hating the rich
as we walk toward the crevices
between children and foreclosed homes

There are dreams of such light
we must dig for them
until decadent pleasures become routine
showers and three coarse meals
and the brightness will diminish us
into phantoms
without guilt

There is a kind of wealth
that is restful
and happy as well
not indolence
but a success story of accidents
striving to be accomplishments
in an increasingly safer world

Sin

I want to sin
weak and tired
the frogs are hopping
behind my eyelids
I don't feel like God is listening
to my ennui
my own attentions are fixed
on the truths beating out of the clock
and the bottle of Hydrocodone on my desk
there are so many violent people
one can meet on the internet
the pastor has stolen our money
to misrepresent himself to the world
he was always so good at
pointing out perversity
despondent I think of the perfect being
with a face smashed in
and all those who delighted in the death
outside Autumn spills its red and orange guts
faced with the harsh interrogations of Winter
we go about our business
under the angelic canopy
selling fine hairs for new skins
there are so many violent people
one can meet on the internet

Customer service

I pen these words
for America. A short poem for a large nation
set to the rhythm of an assembly line.
My grandfather turns the levers
and wheels spin, machines clamor,
steel clashes against steel,
sparks whisper dying chants
before fading into the concrete floor.
My other grandfather
makes his triumphant exhortations in the boardroom
with his trumpet he becomes a master of business
creating dollars and francs in the air.
I am the son of rich and poor
I have a college degree that is of no use to me.
Do the same things anger you?
Let's start a group and meet on Tuesdays,
our swelling outrage will build
into an adagio of idleness. Don't worry,
there is a new game coming out
on PS3. Don't worry,
you can always leave a comment on the internet.
Now that my grandfathers have died
we are stuck working in customer service.
Rude people paid to not be rude
to rude people whom we will enjoy being rude to
once they go to work.

Blue azaleas

The college men
always came around
you had the best weed back then
we would sit in your room for hours
scavenging through the sounds of records
for the belongings of the dead
in this room
I was alone and with you
I used to hate you for all the men you had
dancing and singing
until the doorbell rang
we never kissed
in the months when stares
seemed to foretell blue azaleas
blooming in the black braids of our buoyancy
many years later
we had sex
after you slept with all my friends and enemies
and we were too old for forgetting
you were never
going to find love
in anything that could fit inside a condom
and those nights when you left me
for the overly apologetic menagerie
in the Department of Literature
you would embrace me
your cruel departures were always more amorous
than your entrances

Pocatello, ID

Once old town vomited a railroad
that drained out to the prairie
with all the digested remains of the voting booth
crack pipes and newspapers
lying in sagebrush
now townsfolk talk to the old town
in an abandoned factory
he must maintain the illusion
of fast food palaces
on the main strip
the Portneuf runs through
crying out "America!!!"
crying out "Liberty!!!"
crying out "Poetry!!!"
with bits of shrapnel in its lungs
only some can hear it
over the diesel engines of cowboys
the gangsta rap of the teenagers
the sirens of obsessively vigilant police
one night we follow our forebears to the factory
all the ghosts living and dead
who work in offices or smoky bars
we hide behind a machine
and see the old town
wearing a turtleneck
in the center of the crowd
his long blond hair tied into a ponytail
he sticks his fingers in his throat
but nothing ever comes out

Faith

It's hard for me
to listen to you pray,
were these the prayers spoken by the Christians

who killed off
so many Indians?
Likewise I am filled with pensive thoughts when the pastor

speaks about grace.
I don't know what that is
in this room where everyone is afraid to laugh

with the force of
robins snatching whispers
from streetlight revelations. The woman with the eyes

of a pine tree
planted in the desert is speaking
with the man whose voice has been dismembered

by the verbal surgeons
of the public transportation system.
Two men are engaged in a competition of Bible verses.

I want to run away
from this diet of goat milk
and bleach but something I don't know still calms me.

Prostitute

In Prague I had sex with a prostitute
it was legal there or maybe just not illegal there
after my date spurned me
I rode the subway
for hours, through all the different neighborhoods
searching for the waitress who had left me waiting
in the Old Town Square with the tourists and their riches
I wept with rage and shame until I found the mistake
that I had been trying for years to accomplish
a beautiful Slovakian
dancing for me in a golden room
filled with mirrors and champagne
and when I pleaded for sex
mouthing prayers into panties
she took me to a different room with a broken television and a
fluorescent light flickering
clothes lying everywhere, cigarette butts on the floor
she demanded I shower and when I came out of the bathroom
shivering, I noticed that doctors had gathered around the bed
where she lay naked
there were machines set up to monitor my arousal
while nurses administered condoms and lube
she mounted me and began speaking
in Latin, naming diseases
while shouting orders to the doctors for nipple clamps
and more lube
and more lube
until I was submerged and she was left humping an island
she climbed off of me, the doctors made an incision
and I bled the green worms of depravity
that formed a colony in the great lake of lube

Preservation

It's late and you're in bed
mourning the things we said tonight
bone cry, semen of the tiger
Lenin is still preserved somewhere
and every minute we argue
is an infected waterfall
one day my father will die
taking so many stories with him
tales never told or anecdotes I can't recall
but all the beatings I suffered
will still be here with me
there is more I need to keep
so I will prolong him with poetry
stretching his red cheeks on the page
with the terrain of a distant planet
spreading his yellow teeth with the ears of corn
that grow in the cold Nebraska of your imagination
I will preserve a fingernail in this poem
maybe a strand of hair
while the rest is lost in a grave
that I will one day go to
beautiful, as you lie in bed
celebrities are aging on camera
sex symbols reduced to rubble
these walls will not record our laughter
even these lines may fade with us
my body burns toward death
yet I feel no pain
our souls unified in this instant
as I lay down next to you

Upon the face of the waters

Underneath the sunset
of pink running her fingers
along the rectum of gray
souls gather
looking for meaning on the shoreline
the steel sun is rusting
sinking to the bottom of the sea
cars rush past
units moving units towards units
where they keep their belongings
I am terrified this night
elephants move between rain drops
seals travel thousands of miles
upon waters of wind
God is taking my youth
each unit I surround myself with
is emasculating me
into a smaller unit
none of us understand the deal
that He has arranged around our pleasures
last Thanksgiving I cooked my first turkey
as my expectant in-laws
sat scowling in the adjoining room
begrudgingly they ate the meal I placed before them
I thought it tasted great
but none of us said anything

Appetizer: Morsels of my Dysfunction

Benjamin Schmitt

Smartphone

My smartphone and I have daddy issues,
we discuss them
as I touch his screen. The smartphone
has solved so many of my problems
that I would like to stop this mockery of gigabytes
but I have no app to offer him.
Likewise he has no directions on this highway
where any town could be my birthplace.
The road signs here
remind me of mistakes
20 Miles to your Last Attempted Suicide.
We ask each other what we can do
when cruelty is a download.
Guilt has been dried out in this desert
far from the sea that whispers my name,
its skins tied to fences
blowing in scarred breezes.
I roll down my window
to raise my cellphone up
he searches for a signal but what we really want
is maybe.

Beach

This beach is a suicide
sand and towels the outstretched hands
dripping life into the foam
forget your Quaalude nightmares
shore of the heaving breast
and the eyes looking towards the hearse
driving clouds through the welkin
the ocean will forever drift in the silence
of your many deaths
a tempest arrives
lightning flashes above the broken boardwalk

Punk Show

Gathered in basements
of carpet and booze
we listened to bands
who owned nothing but their instruments
and the vans they drove to town in.
The music swung
at music, not violently
but like a pendulum. Boots stained
the glorious puke of dawn
when something like love beckoned us.
Elephants of t-shirts and cassette tapes
bound together with chains
had conversations about the future of toilet paper.
A few minutes ago
the bus passed by
while I was tracking it on my phone,
now I have missed it
and I need to tell you that part of me
will always be at a punk show in Idaho
pushing myself violently
between guitar and bass. There are currents
shadows have only glimpsed at. Music drifts
upon diaphanous plates of light
there is always someone
who doesn't get it.

I am happy as long as you are happy

In this melancholy
the day is distant
a neighbor down the hall
who wears annoying sweaters
made of clocks
avoiding him
because I was fired
I won't get unemployment
for another three weeks
I am happy as long as you are happy
is what the day
has always told me
but in my despondency
he doesn't even smile at me in the hall
it is apparent the phrase
I am happy as long as you are happy
is a phrase spoken in resignation
the sadness of a democratic life
but maybe this is his sanity
the day with the dusk-red hair
and hazel eyes
filled with golden jams of traffic
I am happy as long as you are happy
and I also enjoy the sorrow

Shale

The rage so deep
it is the foundation and the cave
and the trembling is your whole life living

Some look for shale
breaking under the lightest of hammer strokes
into sleek thin shards of sensitivity

We crack outside
mountainous magnificence the wine glass
through which we spelunk our own explorers

Wild rocks of red
formidable walls of fragmented stone
snowy peaks splintered before touching the yellow sky

Elba

This is a poem I found
in an apple fritter at four a.m., found
at a twenty four hour donut shop
workers shaking
from the combination
of methamphetamines and donuts
taking a sip of coffee I watch the rain
as it dives naked into the street lights
customers come in drunk
and I'm envious
the women hold each other
the men take everything they can before morn
all I have is this poem found
in an apple fritter at four a.m., found
in the rain, in all the
dead presidents
this poem is the knife
that kisses the wrists
here on Elba
Napoleon is reaching for war
planning battles in the sand
there are so many soldiers out there
but all he has is this poem found
in an apple fritter at four a.m., found
just a few miles
off the coast of the world

Womb

There is a kind of slow nightmare
that goes on for so long
the monotonous series of defeats
calls itself a victory. Perhaps it makes the assertion
because you do not feel certain fears or pains
but in truth you are protected
in a madwoman's womb
where the placenta is the heavily accented voice
of a bicycle. It can last longer than nine months
or less than nine days
but you will never know
attached to such umbilical boredom. Inside her belly,
apart from God and time,
you create a routine out of discarded materials like
tragedies, depravities, seashells, or nightcrawlers.
I fashioned mine
from G.I. Joe action figures
and the caring rage
of a breakdown. Later I was born
in the aisles of an anarchist bookstore
surrounded by cynical clerks
in a city I have never known. An old poet
was talking to a young poet about modern sex toys,
the young poet answered in dactylic hexameter.

Absent parent

On these summer days of bikinis and traffic jams,
when the bloodied youth climb out of the asphalt
to take their revenge
upon the humidity (a tourist with heavy suitcases
dragging the rest of us down)
I only want you, a bratwurst,
and the shade of a tree
on the mayor's estate
after we have trespassed on his lawn.
The sun has been a wild, absent parent,
a deadbeat dad who just showed up out of nowhere
trying to make up for his carousing abroad.
Does he want to make us into Mercury,
burned out and not allowed to grow on our own?
The moons of Uranus are waiting out there
cold and abandoned
while Jupiter beats his wife. In his eye a storm of anxiety rages
as he watches us from behind the curtain of distance
in his trailer adjoining the asteroid field.
But the sun is here and maybe he loves us
as I love you
and your legs that curve like solar flares
evaporating into breaths.
There is no literary merit in suicide
but that does not stop them on these eviscerating days.

Terraforming

How I miss you body gone head not on
my shoulder you took my clothes I run
naked down streets without you
pursued by cops
and Seattleites who believe this is a new fad
they want to break us
up so they can keep running naked
forever I am a Martian
terrain filled with traces of your soothing
only able to be explored
at great expense to the federal government
millions of years ago your atmosphere
formed around me rocks
eroded by wet kisses as I was shaped into something
that resembles you terraforming breath
star of God space is floating

Water

You can feel so sad
that your smile is infectious
all of your hidden feelings
leaping into other hearts
until breakfast disappears into nothing
and the clock is only able to tell the latitude
and longitude of a memory
the windows of your house
become the windows of an airplane
as you look out upon a city you've never seen before
filled with the sad people
you want nothing to do with
infected by you their taxicabs
float upwards into the air
they are coming after you
to itch their rashes
you barricade yourself in the bathtub
because the dirty water is the only mess
you can control at thirty thousand feet
the lay minister shouts at you from the mirror
surrounded by the housewives
who are still trying to claim you
your skin surrounds water
and water surrounds you
the sadness in your heart
is never seen at dinner

A Salad of Hope
and Lima Beans

Surgery

The doctor is cutting her open
again, because the scalpel missed her.
I fight with the scalpel
for possession of her flesh,
he has left his long permanent kisses upon her.
The scalpel will always win
he has a team of medical experts
validating all of his caresses. She has my love,
claimed to cause violent parenthetical cursing
by an anonymous blogger,
now the doctors must remove it. They pull some out,
it is made of that shrinking substance
with which we have accepted every tragedy.
But her body is brave like the universe is brave
and love can only expand
from such violence.

Patients

Patients, we need patience,
we need love. Horses galloping
out of daffodils
running towards lush archipelagos

of time. Patients, we are
stricken, lovers sliced open,
we bleed into
each other, your organs fall into me,

I push my intestines apart.
Patients, in our hospital gowns,
everyone can see
our different colored asses from

behind. They see my fingers
surround your wrist across
sicknesses and races.
Patients, we only glimpsed marble,

outside the high fences
of antiquated academies.
Patients, we take our
medicine, pills and bonded sadness.

Oh night

Oh night of sheets falling upon flashlight skyscrapers
underneath we tell ghost stories through advertising

Oh night of the monarch conferring a sense of mystery
even a peasant gains majesty on a dimly lit sidewalk

Oh night of a hundred moons spreading democracy
over fields and glens your constitutions are blazing

Oh night of the soldier running from the surprise attack
only safe in the lengthening shadows that terrify

Oh night of the newlyweds slipping off their clothes
her nervous body prepared with fragrances and glitter

Oh night of the homeless man who went to Harvard
pushing his wife to McDonald's in a shopping cart

Oh night of the stab victim recovering on a gurney
struggling to understand the English of the nurses

Oh night of the Labrador old and lying down to sleep
shuddering on the rug in disapproval of bluebirds

Oh night of UFO lights zipping over cows and farmers
and the beds where we cuddle with extraterrestrials

Country roads

The long country roads I grew up on
were tattoos on the backs of the fields
indecipherable ancient scripts
written for scholarly stars
violets and celandines grew in ditches
bales of hay encircled into henges
John Deere tractors loomed nearby
keeping watch over the rotting hay
sometimes I would stop my bike
just to exist with these bales
in the kind of stillness that attracts flies
until the shouting sun would stir me
to keeping riding toward the imaginations of the cows
imaginations of shit and electric fences
black continents surrounded by oceans of milk
passing through this
with my own dreams of swords and chivalry
eventually I would find a forest
that encouraged my boyish games
where trees whispered to stars
attempting to translate
the mysteries of the roads

Weirdos

I even love the nerdy things about you
especially the nerdy things
your Captain American action figure
and the time you wore socks and sneakers
along with that fancy black dress.
Those reality show stars you know by name
and the stories you have of meeting them in person.
That time we watched the symphony perform Handel's Messiah,
you brought your own book of music
to follow along,
the music reverberated around us
as you read the notes floating upon the air.

The times when I'm a nerd and you still love me:
discussing robot/human marriage
a contentious issue in the year 2315,
The times when I flail my body to "Love is a Battlefield"
performing something that might resemble dancing
slapping my chest and throwing my hair all around.
The way I feel in a bookstore,
the silence of being surrounded by voices
and the expectation of pleasure
the breath before that first sip of coffee in the morning.

The times when we're nerds together:
our *Lord of the Rings* marathon,
holding each other close
and cheering our hobbits on.
The way you mispronounce the word Italian
just like I do
as if to single out that first letter
and make it an individual apart
from the world's pretentiousness.
Our date in that park at night

holding hands as shadows came out of bushes
and noises chased us down a dirt path.
The times when we discuss comic books
as the rain falls down outside the cheap restaurant
that never takes down their Christmas lights
and has delicious chimichangas.
You tell me about the importance of Spiderman
and his relevance to the modern world
somehow I always find a way to bring up *The Matrix*
our eyes meet as I drink my Mexican beer.

Romantic comedies

Pour a glass of wine
and I will tell you about my total psychological
disintegration. The time I spent inside a nuclear bomb
splitting hairs with an atom.
The sun is out and so is everyone in Seattle,
breathing in the warm sighs of a woman
losing her virginity. Can I criticize the sun
as he makes his awkward way
slapping high fives with cloudy pontiffs?
We'll keep tearing down the conventions of honesty
until we are no longer talking, confessing our secrets
with eye movements and grunts.
Sometimes I just want to jam a needle in my arm
and then needle a jam onto a political slogan.
Raspberry dripping from needling eyes.
More than that I want to watch
romantic comedies with you.
The kind where the lead actress meets the man she can't stand
and gradually falls in love despite the obstacles
of everything about him. They say this is what love is
and I for one believe the box office returns
and the way your head fits upon my shoulder
as we are watching them.
Let's close the blinds on this Spring day,
I will make some popcorn
and together we will stare at the ornate frames
of our best feet forward.

Newlyweds

Let me touch
the floor of the pool
where I swim holding love
as bubbles of it escape from me.

Let me swallow
capsules of insults
dissolving into used cars
driving unforgettably from my lot.

Let me drift
through experiences
old songs jutting from hillsides
old men approaching whom I don't know.

Let me look
into jazz trumpet
eyes ringing out across
the midnight lounge of my failings.

Let me massage
your back and neck
and back to unemployment
back to eating ramen noodles for breakfast.

Let me listen
to your humiliations
I have had so many of my own
whistles crashing into overbearing skies.

Dough

I am in awe of that rolling laugh
which has flattened the dough of my emotional outbursts.
A rebel,
I once cherished my lumpy mass,
now I long for a cheek pressed tightly against the cutting board.
Your laugh consists of a billion dimples
which fell to earth as meteorites
many ages ago. The meteorites landed
in a cool mountain lake.
Shaped by the calm certainty
of the reflected peak, they were collected
by a lost and despondent regiment of Confederate soldiers
and somehow they have passed down to you.
Our bitter world
governed by scientific laws
of failure and mortality
also contains your laugh of stars
in all its palpable brilliance,
Polyphemus chasing us through fire.

Button *for Aaron*

My youth was spent
suffering from fantasies
of old age, lonely as I communicated
with the mocking world.
Now I live for
a single button
inside an enormous and otherwise empty chest
surrounded by a shadowy thicket.
Birds call out in the night,
drunks ramble,
the moon takes a swing at me
for joking about his mother.
My hope is in the button
plain and plastic.
It is all that is left.
Through the holes of this button
I weave my loss
until I have designed a garment.
This clothing
brought to my muse,
most gifted tailor,
she takes the measurements
and fits every inch
until an aspect of the glory, power, and humility appears
but only for a moment can these threads
contain the semblance.
The form disappears,
the button endures beside me.
My hope is in the button.

Runner

I see you as the wine pours faces
when the sun has not yet won supremacy
as revelers and addicts
retreat to their beds
still fighting

in their spent way
to keep the glinting lights
on their shoulders. Runner,
you are the dream of queens

in the time of the purple sidewalks
when funk music beats through
your headphones.

You are a planet
burnt to the core,
Mercury in its track around the sun
wearing winged shoes

of ashes.
I would like to meet you

just once
every day for the next seven years
before I cry into a tomato
and we must live the distance
of intimacy. Let us be strangers

in love in some cheap hotel lobby
in Las Vegas at five a.m.
You can soothe me with the caffeine promises of day,
and I will share the serenity of street lights
as the night is fading.

Snow song *for Pete and Nancy*

In Wisconsin snow arrives in October
the wind screams
houses bare icicle fangs against it
clouds smother with love
billions of kisses adorn the land
the clothes of a crazed lover
I would trek through these deep snows
with long lunging strides
leaving my footprints in the drifts
as I tried to keep my balance in an awkward snowsuit
exhalations were the mediums
summoning the wispy ghosts of winter
and I was a princeling of the north
standing knee deep in crystals
looking back at the lights of the farmhouse
across those fields
where lone stalks of wheat would pass through
searching for a summer

Dock of glass

Do you remember that night on the beach
when the ocean receded
into a shell of wind
creating a dock of glass that
reflected all the incongruous musings
of the moonlight?
We could see boats on the horizon,
green and red lights
climbing a yellow wall with steel fingers
to shout their stories
across the mysterious Pacific.
Walking out just far enough
to see the waves still crashing in,
we held each other tight
on the precarious dock
where puerility was shimmering.
This magical extension
between sea and shore
was filled with the translucent footsteps
of the nymphs who tended it. Looking back
towards the shore I saw
our friends gathered around the campfire.
The territory we had claimed was fleeting
like the night, like the boats, like the Pacific,
everything would be different
in the morning.

T.

As we listened to Mozart on her couch
I felt so light
as the pleading and then indifferent
sounds swirled around us.

I lost my bones and my face blew to dust
during the overture,
sweeping me up, she gathered me
from the corners and crevices

of her living room. I rediscovered my body
in her arms. As she
clutched me I felt the music of pores
singing through skin and I knew

that to truly love the music one had to be
reborn in such embraces,
to experience the inevitability of total loss
before sensing the fluidity.

Her hair streaked across my jacket like rays
of light chasing
surreptitious shadows, her head lay
on my chest. It was

her perfume that anointed me in the thick oils
of the masterpiece.
It smelled of lavender and chocolate as I breathed
lives upon her neckline.

Evolution

I lie naked thinking about you
thinking about you lying naked
after our date I wanted
to dive beneath your surface of clothes
filling my lungs with ocean
seaweed wrapping itself around
as sharks nibble on the toes
of my corpse swirling in sunlight
I am the eager diver
who has not yet touched the water
wishing for a suicidal swim so I can dissolve
into your transatlantic currents of breasts
you are so far from the cancer
that covered everything in an oil spill slick
there are depths beyond the fish of your body
deep sea creatures scavenging on the bottom
with grotesque features
maybe my flesh will bring them to the surface
and eventually to land
one act of hunger
begetting an entire species

Benjamin Schmitt

Acknowledgements

The author gratefully acknowledges the editors of the following publications where these poems first appeared:

Belleville Park Pages- Shapes
Black Heart Magazine- Sea Monster
Blue Lyra Review- We were radicals
Drunk Monkeys- The veranda
Exercise Bowler- T.
Forth- Khrushchev
Futures Trading- Pocatello, ID and Refuge
Grist- Runner
Hobart- That night
Marco Polo- Patients and Impotent
Matter- Political ad
Packingtown Review- July 4th, 2012
Pennsylvania Literary Journal- Sonnet #10, White guilt, and Dough
Penny Ante Feud- Broken Marriage
Poplorish- The fiery planet
Potluck- Sonnet #3 and Water
Poydras Review- Music of our fathers
Qua- Fake Christians
River Poets Journal- Womb
Sakura Review- Table
Seltzer- Absent parent and Trans
SNReview- Advice
Star*Line- ROBOT UPRISING!!! and Alternate history
Stepaway Magazine- On the bus, January 1st, 2012
Storyacious- Legend of a perfume
The Monarch Review- The bookshelf and Smartphone
The Muse- Country roads
Torrid Literature Journal- Button
Triggerfish Critical Review- Oh night and Surgery
Two Thirds North- Political ad and Prayer
Wisconsin Review- My application and Punk Show
Work Literary Magazine- Customer service and On wealth
Works and Days Quarterly- 1997 and Herbert Schmitt

Made in the USA
Middletown, DE
19 April 2016